SandCastle™

First Rhymes

Adell and the Secret Well

Anders Hanson

Consulting Editor, Diane Craig, M.A./Reading Specialist

ABDO
Publishing Company

Published by ABDO Publishing Company, 4940 Viking Drive, Edina, Minnesota 55435.

Printed in the United States.

Credits
Edited by: Pam Price
Curriculum Coordinator: Nancy Tuminelly
Cover and Interior Design and Production: Mighty Media
Photo Credits: AbleStock, Eyewire Images, Photodisc, Stockbyte, Wewerka Photography

Library of Congress Cataloging-in-Publication Data

Hanson, Anders, 1980-
    Adell and the secret well / Anders Hanson.
        p. cm. -- (First rhymes)
    Includes index.
    ISBN 1-59679-447-X (hardcover)
    ISBN 1-59679-448-8 (paperback)
    1. English language--Rhyme--Juvenile literature. I. Title. II. Series.
PE1517.H3 2005
808.1--dc22
                                                                                    2005048043

SandCastle™ books are created by a professional team of educators, reading specialists, and content developers around five essential components that include phonemic awareness, phonics, vocabulary, text comprehension, and fluency. All books are written, reviewed, and leveled for guided reading and early intervention reading, and designed for use in shared, guided, and independent reading and writing activities to support a balanced approach to literacy instruction.

Let Us Know

After reading the book, SandCastle would like you to tell us your stories about reading. What is your favorite page? Was there something hard that you needed help with? Share the ups and downs of learning to read. We want to hear from you! To get posted on the ABDO Publishing Company Web site, send us e-mail at:

sandcastle@abdopub.com

SandCastle Level: Beginning

-ell

bell

cell

shell

well

yell

This is a .

We see a  .

I see the  .

Here is the  .

I can  .

The bell is silver.

The cell is small.

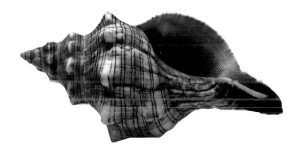

The shell is pretty.

A well has water.

Greg likes to yell.

Adell and the Secret Well

A girl named Adell
finds a secret well.

Above the well
is a big bell.

18

When Adell
rings the bell,
she hears a yell
from inside the well!

Out of the well
with a bell
comes a genie
in a shell.

Adell hears him yell,
"I am the big Montell!"

"I heard you yell,"
  says Adell.

"Were you stuck
  in the well?"

"Yes," says Montell.

"When I hear
  that big bell,
  I come out of my shell!"

About SandCastle™

A professional team of educators, reading specialists, and content developers created the SandCastle™ series to support young readers as they develop reading skills and strategies and increase their general knowledge. The SandCastle™ series has four levels that correspond to early literacy development in young children. The levels are provided to help teachers and parents select the appropriate books for young readers.

Emerging Readers
(no flags)

Beginning Readers
(1 flag)

Transitional Readers
(2 flags)

Fluent Readers
(3 flags)

These levels are meant only as a guide. All levels are subject to change.

To see a complete list of SandCastle™ books and other nonfiction titles from ABDO Publishing Company, visit **www.abdopub.com** or contact us at: 4940 Viking Drive, Edina, Minnesota 55435 • 1-800-800-1312 • fax: 1-952-831-1632